C0-BIG-490

EYE to EYE with ANIMALS

AMAZING APES

by Ruth Owen

WINDMILL BOOKS

New York

Published in 2013 by Windmill Books, An Imprint of Rosen Publishing
29 East 21st Street, New York, NY 10010

Copyright © 2013 by Windmill Books, An Imprint of Rosen Publishing

All rights reserved. No part of this book may be reproduced in any form without permission in writing from the publisher, except by a reviewer.

Produced for Windmill by Ruby Tuesday Books Ltd
Editor for Ruby Tuesday Books Ltd: Mark J. Sachner
US Editor: Sara Antill
Designer: Emma Randall

Photo Credits:
Cover, 15 © Corbis; 1, 4–5, 7, 8–9, 11, 12–13, 16–17, 19, 20–21, 24, 25 (top), 27, 28–29 © Shutterstock; 23, 25 (bottom) Superstock.

Library of Congress Cataloging-in-Publication Data

Owen, Ruth, 1967–
Amazing apes / by Ruth Owen.
    p. cm. — (Eye to eye with animals)
Includes index.
ISBN 978-1-4488-8067-6 (library binding) — ISBN 978-1-4488-8103-1 (pbk.) —
ISBN 978-1-4488-8109-3 (6-pack)
1. Apes—Juvenile literature. I. Title.
QL737.P96O838 2013
599.88—dc23

                              2012009193

Manufactured in the United States of America

CPSIA Compliance Information: Batch # B2S12WM: For Further Information contact Windmill Books, New York, New York at 1-866-478-0556

CONTENTS

Meet the Apes!

They have long arms, hairy bodies, no tails, and they are very, very smart. Meet the apes!

Apes belong to an animal group known as **primates**. The primate group includes apes, **monkeys**, and **prosimians**, which are small animals such as bushbabies and lemurs.

The smartest of all the primates are the great apes. Orangutans, chimpanzees, gorillas, and bonobos are all known as great apes. In this book, we'll be taking a close-up look at their lives. We'll also be meeting gibbons, which are known as lesser apes.

There's one extremely smart great ape, however, that won't be featured in this book. You already know a lot about this clever creature, though, because it's you! Humans are also great apes and are the smartest of all the primates.

An adult and young gorilla

4

APES IN DANGER

Sadly, humans have not taken good care of their ape cousins. All **species**, or types, of ape are **endangered**. Apes are hunted by people, and their **habitat**, the **rain forests** of Africa and Southeast Asia, are being destroyed.

CHIMPANZEES
The Smartest Apes

Height (when standing on back legs):
3.3 to 5.6 feet (1–1.7 m)

Weight: 57 to 154 pounds (26–70 kg)

Weight at birth: 4.4 pounds (2 kg)

Lifespan: 40 to 60 years

Breeding age (females): 10 to 13 years

Breeding age (males): 12 to 15 years

Diet: Plants, fruit, nuts, honey, insects, and small animals

Habitat: Forests in Africa. Chimpanzees spend time on the ground and in trees.

FACE FACTS

Chimpanzees make faces at each other as a way of communicating, or talking. They also use body movements and sounds, such as screams, hoots, and panting noises. They mix up noises and faces in different ways to mean different things.

Adult chimpanzee

7

Chimpanzees are the smartest of all the apes. They live in groups that may have 20 members, or as many as 100!

Teamwork and Tools

Chimps spend their days looking for food. Sometimes male chimps work as a team to chase and catch monkeys, wild pigs, and antelopes. Smart chimps also use tools to find and prepare food. They like to eat termites, which are insects that live in large mud nests. A chimp will poke a stick into a termite nest. When some termites climb onto the stick, the chimp pulls the stick from the nest and eats the insects.

Chimpanzee Mothers

A female chimp gives birth to one baby at a time. She feeds the baby milk until it is about two years old. She teaches the baby which plants and other foods are good to eat. Mother chimps care for their babies until they are about six years old.

A chimpanzee with a termite "fishing stick"

TICKLES, HUGS, AND KISSES

Just like people, chimps kiss and hug their friends and family members. They also like to tickle and be tickled!

A baby chimpanzee

Endangered Chimpanzees

Chimpanzees are seriously endangered. About 100 years ago, there were one million wild chimps in Africa. Today, there are fewer than 300,000.

Chimps are hunted by people for food, even though it is against the law.

Chimps are taken from the forest to be sold as pets.

The forests where the chimps live and find their food are cut down for lumber.

CHIMPANZEES RANGE MAP

AFRICA

The red areas on the map show where chimpanzees live wild.

ORANGUTANS
The Largest Tree-Living Animals on Earth

Height (when standing on back legs):
   3.3 to 5 feet (1–1.5 m)

Weight (female): **66 to 110 pounds (30–50 kg)**

Weight (male): **110 to 220 pounds (50–100 kg)**

Weight at birth: **3.3 pounds (1.5 kg)**

Lifespan: **40 to 60 years**

Breeding age (females): **15 years**

Breeding age (males): **10 - 14 years**

Diet: **300 types of fruit. Plants, mushrooms, insects and spiders, eggs, and sometimes small animals**

Habitat: **Rain forests on the islands of Borneo and Sumatra, in Southeast Asia**

FACE FACTS

An adult male orangutan tries to become the boss of an area in the forest. He then gets to **mate** with the females in that area. He makes loud calls and grows large cheek pads that show other males he's the boss!

Adult male orangutan

11

Orangutans live high in rain forest trees, up to 100 feet (30.5 m) above the ground.

Smart Food Finders

Adult orangutans usually live alone. They spend their days climbing and swinging through the treetops looking for food. An orangutan's **territory**, or home area, may be as large as 700 football fields. The orangutan knows every tree in the area, and when each tree's fruit will be **ripe** and ready to eat. Orangutans also use rain forest plants as medicines to treat headaches and upset stomachs.

Caring Mothers

A female orangutan has one baby at a time. The baby rides on its mother's body, holding onto her long hair. Mother orangutans feed their babies milk until they are about five years old. They teach their babies how to climb and what foods to eat and use as medicines. A mother orangutan cares for her baby until it is about nine years old.

An orangutan eating fruit

SMART PROBLEM SOLVERS

Smart orangutans use leaves as protective gloves when holding fruit with spiky skins. They also use leaves as napkins to wipe their faces.

A mother orangutan and her baby, high in the rain forest trees

Endangered Orangutans

There are around 60,000 wild orangutans left on Earth. They are seriously endangered!

The rain forests where orangutans live are cut down for lumber and for wood to be made into paper.

The forests are burned down so that farmers can grow palm oil trees. The oil from these plants is used in foods and makeup.

Thousands of female orangutans have been killed so that their babies can be kidnapped and sold as pets.

ORANGUTANS RANGE MAP

ASIA

Malaysia

Borneo

Sumatra

Indonesia

The red areas on the map show where orangutans live wild.

A four-month-old baby orangutan

GORILLAS
The Largest Apes

Height (when standing on back legs):
  4 to 5.7 feet (1.25–1.75 m)

Weight (female): 150 to 200 pounds (68–91 kg)

Weight (male): 300 to 500 pounds (136–227 kg)

Weight at birth: 4.5 pounds (2 kg)

Lifespan: 35 to 50 years

Breeding age (females): 10 years

Breeding age (males): 15 years

Diet: Plant leaves, stems, roots, seeds, and fruit

Habitat: Rain forests in Africa

FACE FACTS

An adult male gorilla (right) has a very large brow, or forehead. Gorillas have powerful jaws for chewing tough, crunchy plant stems.

Adult male western gorilla

15

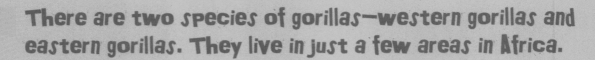

There are two species of gorillas—western gorillas and eastern gorillas. They live in just a few areas in Africa.

Gorilla Troops

Gorillas live in family groups called troops. A troop may have as few as five or as many as 30 members. A gorilla troop is led by an adult male. He is known as a **silverback** because of the silver-colored hair on his back. The silverback is the father of most of the babies in the troop. Each morning, the silverback leads the group to a new place where they spend the day gathering and eating plants.

Gorilla Babies

A female gorilla usually gives birth to one baby at a time. She has her first baby when she is around 10 years old. A baby gorilla rides around on its mother's back. Mother gorillas feed their babies milk and care for them until the babies are three or four years old.

A baby gorilla

16

HUNGRY GORILLAS

Gorillas spend a lot of time each day eating. An adult male gorilla can eat around 40 pounds (18 kg) of food every day!

A baby gorilla riding on its mother's back

An adult male
silverback gorilla

Endangered Western and Eastern Gorillas

Gorillas are seriously endangered! There are only between **15,000** and **20,000** western and eastern gorillas left in the world.

The main threats to gorillas are the loss of their forest habitat and hunting.

Forests are cut down for lumber, leaving the gorillas nowhere to live.

Gorillas are hunted by people as food called bushmeat.

WESTERN AND EASTERN GORILLAS RANGE MAP

The red areas on the map show where gorillas live wild.

MOUNTAIN GORILLAS
Critically Endangered

Height (when standing on back legs):
5 to 6 feet (1.5–1.8 m)

Weight (female): Up to 200 pounds (91 kg)

Weight (male): Up to 400 pounds (181 kg)

Weight at birth: 4.5 pounds (2 kg)

Lifespan: 30 to 40 years

Breeding age (females): 10 years

Breeding age (males): 15 years

Diet: Plants including nettles, thistles, and celery, flowers, bark, roots, berries, and sometimes ants. A favorite food is bamboo.

Habitat: Cold, wet, misty forests on mountains and volcanoes in Africa

FACE FACTS

Every gorilla has a unique pattern of wrinkles on its nose. Scientists who study gorillas take photos of gorillas' noses. They use the "nose prints" to identify who is who in gorilla groups.

Baby mountain gorilla

Mountain gorillas are a type of eastern gorilla. They live in cold forests so they have hair that is longer and thicker than that of other gorillas.

Peaceful Plant Eaters

Mountain gorillas live in small family groups. A group usually has an adult silverback male, three or four adult females and their babies, and several young gorillas. Mountain gorillas spend about half of each day peacefully munching plants. At night, each adult gorilla makes a sleeping nest of leaves and branches in a tree or on the ground.

A mountain gorilla family

A mother gorilla holds her baby to her chest until it is strong enough to hold onto her hair.

Critically Endangered Mountain Gorillas
There are fewer than 800 mountain gorillas left on Earth.

The threats to these gorillas include habitat loss, hunting, and disease. The forests where the gorillas live are cut down by local people for firewood or to make space for growing crops.

People set traps in the forests to catch antelopes and wild pigs. Sometimes mountain gorillas get caught in the traps and die.

Mountain gorillas can catch human diseases and die.

Mothers and Babies
A female mountain gorilla leaves her family when she is around eight years old. She finds a silverback to be her mate and joins his group. A female mountain gorilla gives birth to one baby at a time. She feeds the baby milk, plays with it, and cares for it until it is around four years old. Then she has another baby.

MOUNTAIN GORILLAS RANGE MAP

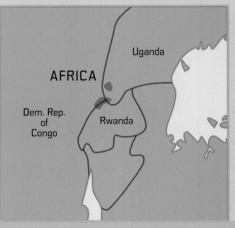

The red areas on the map show the two small, protected forest areas where mountain gorillas live.

GORILLA TALK
Gorillas make low, belching noises, a little like a purr, to show they are happy and content. When a gorilla is afraid it makes roaring and screaming noises.

BONOBOS
The Girls Are in Charge!

Height (when standing on back legs):
Up to 4 feet (1.22 m)

Weight (female): 73 pounds (33 kg)

Weight (male): 100 pounds (45 kg)

Weight at birth: 2.8 pounds (1.3 kg)

Lifespan: up to 50 years

Breeding age (females): 13 to 15 years

Breeding age (males): 13 to 15 years

Diet: Plant leaves and stems, fruit, insects,
and sometimes fish and shrimp.
A favorite food is earthworms.

Habitat: Rain forests in the Democratic
Republic of Congo, Africa

FACE FACTS

Until the 1920s, scientists thought that bonobos were a type of chimpanzee. Now we know they are a completely different species of ape. One way to tell bonobos from chimpanzees is their hairstyle. Bonobos have long hair that parts in the middle!

23

Like chimpanzees and gorillas, bonobos live in groups. In the world of the bonobo, however, the females are in charge!

A Quiet and Happy Life

Bonobos are kind to each other and often touch or hug each other to give comfort. Bonobos live very peacefully and everyone usually gets along. When a young female grows up, she leaves her mother's group and joins a different bonobo group. Males, however, remain living in their mother's group even when they are adults.

Beds and Breakfasts

Bonobos spend their days searching for food on the ground. They also swing from tree to tree to find fruit. Caring bonobos don't fight over the food they find. They share it with their friends. At night, bonobos build nests of leaves and twigs in trees. Often, adult bonobos share a nest. They help keep each other safe at night by keeping watch for **predators** such as snakes and leopards.

Life in a bonobo group can be pretty relaxed!

Bonobos don't mind searching for food in water.

Endangered Bonobos

No one knows for sure how many bonobos are left in the wild, but it is likely to be fewer than 50,000!

The forest habitat of the bonobos is being cut down for lumber.

People hunt bonobos for meat.

Sometimes, baby bonobos are kidnapped to be sold as pets.

BONOBOS RANGE MAP

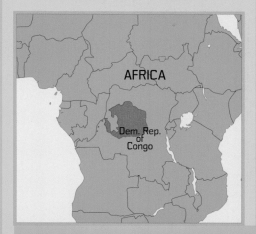

AFRICA

Dem. Rep. of Congo

The red areas on the map show where bonobos live wild.

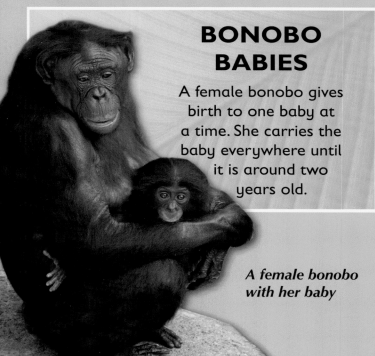

BONOBO BABIES

A female bonobo gives birth to one baby at a time. She carries the baby everywhere until it is around two years old.

A female bonobo with her baby

LAR GIBBONS
The Lesser Apes

Height (when standing on back legs):
2 feet (61 cm)

Weight (female): **11 to 15 pounds (5–7 kg)**

Weight (male): **11 to 15 pounds (5–7 kg)**

Weight at birth: **0.6 pound (300 g)**

Lifespan: **25 to 40 years**

Breeding age (females): **8 years**

Breeding age (males): **8 years**

Diet: **Ripe fruit, new leaves and shoots, flowers, and insects**

Habitat: **Rain forests in Southeast Asia**

FACE FACTS

Lar gibbons are also known as white-handed gibbons. They have a ring of white fur around a dark face, and white hands and feet.

An adult lar gibbon

27

Gibbons are known as lesser apes. There are several different species of gibbons. These slim, very graceful apes are much smaller than all the other ape species.

King of the Swingers

Like all gibbons, lar gibbons have very long arms. They move through the trees by swinging from hand to hand. Gibbons hardly ever come down to the ground. If they do, they run with their long arms above their heads!

A lar gibbon in a zoo shows off the length of its amazing arms!

A lar gibbon shows off its swinging skills.

A female lar gibbon and her baby

Gibbon Families

Lar gibbons live in small families of an adult male, an adult female, and the couple's young. A male and a female gibbon usually stay together for life. Every two to three years, the female gives birth to one baby. She feeds the baby milk until it is about two years old. Young gibbons live with their parents until they are about eight years old.

SINGING GIBBONS

Each lar gibbon pair has a territory in the forest. They keep other gibbons out of their territory by singing a loud, whooping song.

Endangered Gibbons

All gibbon species are endangered and it's difficult for scientists to know for sure how many are left in the wild.

One of the main threats to all gibbons is habitat loss. Their rain forest homes are cut down for lumber or to make space for farms.

Sometimes gibbons are hunted for meat.

Gibbons are also taken from the forest to be sold as pets. Many die during their capture or because they are not properly cared for.

LAR GIBBONS RANGE MAP

The red areas on the map show where lar gibbons live.

GLOSSARY

ape (AYP)
A member of a group of primates that includes gibbons, chimpanzees, bonobos, orangutans, and gorillas. Apes have no tails and most have large bodies. Apes are very intelligent.

endangered (in-DAYN-jerd)
In danger of no longer existing.

habitat (HA-buh-tat)
The place where an animal or plant normally lives. A habitat may be a rain forest, the ocean, or a backyard.

mate (MAYT)
An animal's partner with which it has young; when a male and a female come together in order to have young.

monkey (MUNG-kee)
A member of the primate group of animals, such as a spider monkey or baboon. There are over 250 different types of monkeys. Most monkeys have small bodies and long tails.

predator (PREH-duh-ter)
An animal that hunts and kills other animals for food.

primate (PRY-mayt)
A member of the animal group known as primates. The group includes prosimians, monkeys, apes, and humans. Primates are mammals. They are warm-blooded animals that have backbones and hair, breathe air, and feed milk to their young.

prosimian (pro-SIH-mee-in)
A member of the primate group of animals that includes lemurs and lorises. Prosimians live in forests in Africa, Asia, and on the island of Madagascar.

rain forest (RAYN FOR-est)
A warm, wooded habitat with a lot of rainfall and many types of animals and plants.

ripe (RYP)
When something, such as a fruit or vegetable, is fully formed and ready to eat.

silverback (SIL-ver-bak)
An adult male gorilla that has grown silver hair on his back. A silverback is the leader of a gorilla family, or group.

species (SPEE-sheez)
One type of living thing. The members of a species look alike and can produce young together.

territory (TER-uh-tor-ee)
The area where an animal lives, finds its food, and finds partners for mating.

Websites

For web resources related to the subject of this book, go to: www.windmillbooks.com/weblinks and select this book's title.

READ MORE

Clark, Willow. *Gorillas: Life in the Troop*. Animal Families. New York: PowerKids Press, 2011.

Frost, Helen. *Chimpanzees*. Rain Forest Animals. Mankato, MN: Capstone Press, 2007.

Keller, Susanna. *Meet the Ape*. At the Zoo. New York: PowerKids Press, 2010.

Laman, Tim, and Cheryl Knott. *Face to Face with Orangutans*. Face to Face with Animals. Des Moines, IA: National Geographic Children's Books, 2009.

INDEX